Original title:
Living Under One Roof

Copyright © 2025 Creative Arts Management OÜ
All rights reserved.

Author: Giselle Montgomery
ISBN HARDBACK: 978-1-80587-175-0
ISBN PAPERBACK: 978-1-80587-645-8

The Nest of Our Days

In a house that creaks and moans,
We buy our snacks, we claim our zones.
The sock that vanished, where'd it go?
It's probably joined the laundry show.

With laughter echoing through the air,
We dodge the mess, we don't despair.
The dog will snore, the cat will glare,
Yet somehow, we've formed this weird affair.

The Canvas of Connection

Colors splash on every wall,
With slops and spills, we have a ball.
My paintbrush flies, your hands go wild,
It's chaos, truly, but we're beguiled.

Brushes clash and giggles ring,
We blend our shades like birds that sing.
If life is art, what a fine mess,
Our canvas large, with love, no less.

Embracing Differences

You're a night owl, I greet the dawn,
Your playlist's wild; mine's a soft yawn.
Yet in this dance of quirks and glee,
We find the rhythm, you and me.

Your jokes are dry, like autumn leaves,
I laugh so hard, I can't believe.
It's odd, it's weird, but somehow grand,
In this rainbow, we both stand.

Navigating Together

Maps all over but none in hand,
We wander through the quirky land.
A missing shoe, a funny hat,
We laugh till it hurts, imagine that!

With snacks in pockets, we set out bold,
Searching for treasures, legends told.
In this silly quest, we have our fun,
Together we stumble, together we run.

Unity in Our Journey

In a house where socks always disappear,
We dance around like we have no fear.
One claims the couch, another takes the chair,
Arguing over snacks, but we all share.

Our Quiet Refuge

At times it feels like a circus show,
With pets and kids all on the go.
The fridge is empty, but spirits are high,
We laugh when someone serves a pie.

The Heart of Us

In the chaos, we find our grace,
Whiskers and giggles fill the space.
One sleeps while the other brews tea,
Our home is a puzzle, fits you and me.

Fleeting Moments

Forgotten is the clock on the wall,
Ticking softly in our free-for-all.
A spilled drink becomes a shared joke,
As laughter bursts like an old oak.

Lasting Bonds

When the dust settles, and quiet returns,
Amidst the chaos, my heart still learns.
We may bicker, tease, and sometimes fight,
But united we stand, through day and night.

The Shelter We Share

In a space where socks unite,
And mismatched spoons take flight,
We trip on toys each day,
In a laughable ballet.

The fridge is a puzzle maze,
With leftovers earning praise,
A dance of plates unfolds,
As chaos often holds.

Stories in the Shadows

In the corners, whispers thrive,
Of antics that make us jive,
The dog's snoring, quite the song,
A symphony of cheers so strong.

Cats plotting their mischief spree,
Take bets on who'll catch a bee,
While we gather 'round and grin,
Laughing loud, the tales begin.

Mornings Wrapped in Warmth

Coffee spills in the morning light,
Sneaking bites—oh, what a sight!
Pajamas mixed up in a pile,
We greet the day with quirky style.

Toasts dance with jelly on top,
As we all take a funny flop,
With mouths full, we cannot speak,
Yet laughter shouts out for a week.

A Symphony of Companionship

In our home, a concert plays,
With funny notes through busy days,
The washing machine hums a tune,
While we strut and shake like loons.

We sing in the shower, oh so loud,
As pets join in, feeling proud,
Our quirky band, forever on,
In this sweet, joyful marathon.

The Harmony Within

In the kitchen, chaos reigns,
The dog steals socks, the cat gets grains.
Mom's on a call, dad's in a race,
Can someone find my missing lace?

Dinner's a dance, everyone's late,
We chop and twirl, it's a funny fate.
Spilled the sauce, oh what a scene,
Mom sighs, 'They should've joined a cuisine team!'

On game nights, we yell and cheer,
The scoreboard's wrong, let's blame the beer.
The couch is a fortress, snacks all around,
"Who ate the last chip?" can be quite profound.

Bedtime's a circus, giggles in the air,
The lights go out, but it's hard to care.
With pillows as shields and blankets as capes,
We conquer the night, despite sleep's escapes.

The Fabric of Togetherness

Laundry piles high, what a sight,
Colors and whites, oh what a fright.
Who wore this shirt? It's got a stain,
Mom shakes her head, it's all in vain.

The remote is missing, where could it be?
It's under the couch or stuck in my knee.
The battle for shows, oh what a delight,
"Last time you picked, now it's my night!"

Grocery lists blend from too much fun,
Who bought the pickles? This can't be done.
Each item an adventure, a quirky find,
"Is that vegetable even from our kind?"

The calendar's full, with laughter we plan,
Birthdays and holidays, yes, we can!
In every gathering, chaos meets cheer,
Our house buzzes with joy, year after year.

Portraits of Belonging

Family portraits hang on the wall,
With every smile, we laugh, we fall.
The cat's in the frame, striking a pose,
Next to Uncle Joe, who forgot his clothes.

Each room a story, crammed and bright,
The bathroom's a jungle, a hairdryer fight.
"Who used my towel?" shouts my little sis,
While I'm convinced this is total bliss.

In the evenings we gather, sharing a meal,
Mismatched utensils, that's how we feel.
Talk turns to debates—who's the best cook?
But we all agree it's time for a book.

Hugs at departures, the door's a swing,
"See you tomorrow!" — such joy it brings.
With every chuckle and playful tease,
We find our rhythm, we find our ease.

Shared Spaces

In the fridge, there lies a stash,
Of leftovers, all gone to ash.
A battle of flavors, quite obscene,
Whose ice cream's melting? It's never seen.

Socks in the corner, a laundry pile,
Whose turn is it? Oh, wait a while.
My shirt's mixed up with your old bedspread,
Let's flip a coin, I'll take the dread.

Coasters? What are those, I don't know,
Every cup leaves a mark, oh no!
The couch is a canvas, a pizza stain,
Our lives a puzzle, a little insane.

A Tapestry of Lives

Pants on the doorknob, a sight of dread,
Whose messy life is this? I said!
Each shoe seems to have a dance of its own,
A family of oddities, grown and grown.

Snack wrappers scatter, like confetti tossed,
In this wild home, we all are lost.
A game of skirmish for the couch's throne,
Who gets to rule the remote alone?

Our quirky habits, a strange ballet,
A symphony of chaos in disarray.
But laughter rings loud as we don't quite fit,
In this kooky mess, we're all a bit.

Beneath the Same Ceiling

The thermostat wars are quite absurd,
You're freezing, I'm hot, haven't you heard?
A tug-of-war for the TV remote,
Your show is on? Just let me gloat!

Dishes piled high like a skyscraper,
Whose turn is it? Let's play the caper!
The sink's a river of yesterday's feast,
We'll clean it…but only when we've ceased.

Harmonies of Home

Loud laughter echoes through the hall,
As everyone argues about who's tall.
An orchestra of quirks, of snorts and sighs,
Living together, oh how time flies!

With the cat on the table, and crumbs on the floor,
We've built a community that we adore.
Binge-watching shows till the morning light,
Who knew togetherness could feel so right?

Hearth and Heart

In this cozy space we dwell,
With socks that never quite repel.
The dog steals food right from the plate,
And the cat claims every chair as fate.

Loud laughter echoes off the walls,
While someone trips and gracefully falls.
We dance like no one's watching us,
But oh, that coffee spill was quite a fuss!

Memories Linger Here

In every nook, a memory glows,
Like that time ice cream fell on your nose.
The walls can tell a thousand tales,
Of family dinners and epic fails.

We play board games throughout the night,
A competitive spirit brings delight.
Though someone's always making a cheat,
And snacks are lost to little feet.

The Comfort of Convergence

When breakfast turns to lunch by chance,
We race to finish in a dance.
The kitchen's chaos is quite a sight,
Yet we find joy in every bite.

Genetics might say we're a mixed bag,
But who cares when we laugh and brag?
With voices clashing but hearts in sync,
In chaos, we find our missing link.

A Quilt of Relationships

Stitching together our highs and lows,
Like crafting sweaters with mismatched toes.
From wild debates over TV shows,
To secret recipes no one knows.

Each day we weave through thick and thin,
With playful pranks and cheeky grins.
Our quilt is warm, it never tears,
In this splendid place, love freely shares.

The House That Holds Us

In a house where socks disappear,
The dog hides snacks, oh dear!
The cat's decided it's her throne,
While the kids claim every tone.

Pots and pans like a marching band,
Noisy dinners, a wild stand.
Spilled milk turns into a game,
Who knew chaos could feel so tame?

Bathroom lines stretch like a queue,
"Give me five!" is the morning dew.
Finding peace amid the clatter,
In this mix, we truly matter.

With every laugh, our hearts expand,
Life's a circus, all unplanned.
Together we'll weather rain or shine,
In this messy love, we intertwine.

Kindred Spirits

Three kids bouncing off the walls,
Their laughter echoes through the halls.
A pizza box spins like a dream,
Tossed aside in joyful scream.

The fridge is bare, the pantry's a joke,
Last night's dinner? A leftover yolk.
Chasing crumbs like a wild parade,
Every snack's a hidden crusade.

When the TV's loud and the dog's in place,
Family meetings about personal space.
Yet under it all, a bond so tight,
Even chaos feels incredibly right.

From dawn till dusk, we weave our play,
In this mess, we find our way.
Kindred spirits with hearts so true,
In our nutty house, we break through.

Navigating Our Nest

Navigating through the cluttered maze,
With every room, a different phase.
The laundry's piled, a mountain high,
Who needs a gym? It's do or die!

Voices clash like a lively band,
Every meal a new demand.
Dinner's served with a side of bickering,
But laughter bursts as the clock keeps ticking.

The bathroom wars, oh what a sight,
"Who used the last of the soap tonight?"
Yet in this dance, we all belong,
Even when the chaos feels too strong.

Maps of love drawn in crayon bold,
Our stories shared, our lives unfold.
In this lovely chaos, we jest and cheer,
Navigating life with those we hold dear.

Reflections of Familiarity

In every corner, a memory made,
Life's curiosities on display, unfrayed.
The couch, a fortress, where stories dwell,
Silly secrets we'll never tell.

Giggling over pasta on a Tuesday night,
Is it burning? Well, that feels just right.
Spilled stories on a well-worn floor,
Every mishap opens a new door.

The hallway echoes with silly tunes,
Dancing shadows from the morning moons.
Even the walls know our daily stress,
Yet they whisper comfort in our mess.

Through ups and downs, we find our song,
In this shared space, we all belong.
In our laughter, tears, and shared delights,
The truth of us shines in all our fights.

Voices in the Hallway

Voices echo, playful sounds,
Laughter travels 'round and 'round.
Footsteps shuffle, dance a beat,
Who stole my sandwich? Oh, what a feat!

Pranks and games, we love to tease,
Someone's lost a sock or keys.
Dinner bell rings, what a feast!
Who hid the dessert? Not the least!

Unity in Diversity

Colors clash but hearts are bright,
Silly hats, a strange delight.
A mix of cultures, spice and fun,
Who knew that broccoli could outrun?

We share the space, we share the jokes,
Mismatched socks and goofy blokes.
In our chaos, we find a tune,
Dancing 'neath the bright, round moon.

Bonds in the Breeze

Windows open, breezy sighs,
Chasing kites and silly flies.
A cat that pounces, dogs that bark,
Watch out for the leap, oh dear, it's stark!

We're tangled up in laughter's spree,
Who borrowed my book? Oh, wait, it's me!
Our hearts are tied, a playful crew,
With each little mess, we start anew.

The Dance of Daily Life

Morning rush and coffee spills,
Toothpaste battles, laughter fills.
Chasing socks that hide away,
Living life in a funny ballet.

Evenings filled with karaoke dreams,
Dishwashers hum, and laughter gleams.
We twist and twirl, a wacky grind,
In this circus, joy's what we find!

Echoes of Togetherness

In the kitchen, we do the dance,
Spilling coffee, but never a chance.
Who took the last slice of that pie?
We laugh and we wonder, oh my, oh my.

To each their own, we claim our space,
Yet trip on shoes, a chaotic race.
With every door, there's a mystery,
What's that noise? Just our history.

Pillow fights like stormy weather,
Apologies come, we mend together.
The fridge is our shared battleground,
Rescue the leftovers before they drown.

Laughter rings like chimes in the air,
Our quirky ways show how much we care.
Through ups and downs, we always find,
Home's a mess, but love is kind.

Walls That Whisper

In the hallways, gossip takes flight,
Whispers echoing deep in the night.
What's that smell? Is it burnt toast?
Chef's hat worn by the one we roast.

Colors clash in the living space,
Not a single thing has a proper place.
Remote control hid in a sea of socks,
Under the couch, the mystery rocks.

Funny faces in the bathroom mirror,
Toothpaste battles, we hold dearer.
Squeaky floors moan as we run,
Who knew sharing a roof could be such fun?

Each corner, a tale, each room, a song,
In this big circus, we all belong.
With laughter loud and friendships tight,
Our walls, they whisper through day and night.

Unison in the Everyday

Breakfast time, what's that sound?
Sibling warfare, the crumbs abound.
Who gets the last egg? A fierce showdown,
But in this chaos, we wear the crown.

Laundry day, a colorful fight,
Whose socks are these? A puzzling sight.
With every spin, laughter appears,
Dodge the pile, we play with our fears.

TV shows bring our family crew,
Shouting lines, it's a team debut.
Popcorn flies, as tension grows,
A minute's silence, then mayhem flows.

In every routine, we find our fun,
Dancing together 'til the day is done.
Shared rhythms make our hearts sway,
In this wild ensemble, we find our way.

A Tapestry of Lives

A patchwork quilt of love and cheer,
Threads intertwine through every year.
Each stitch tells a tale, each tear a laugh,
In our crazy quilt, we share the craft.

Dinner's chaos with forks that clash,
Pass the peas, or they'll make a splash.
Who's on dish duty? Not today, my friend,
Debates and smiles with no clear end.

Snoring symphonies fill the night,
In slumber, we're a comical sight.
Dreams collide in a colorful mix,
While pillow forts protect our tricks.

Every moment adds to the plot,
Life in this circus connects the dots.
With humor and joy, we weave and spin,
In this grand tapestry, we always win.

Homebound Harmony

In this house, socks disappear,
The fridge has snacks we revere.
Couch cushions tossed, a fort takes shape,
Two cats scheme, while kids escape.

Dinner's served with a side of brawl,
Who stole the last roll? There's always a call.
Laughter echoes, chaos reigns,
Yet love remains, even with stains.

Moments in the Living Room

The TV blares, a jungle of noise,
Remote control? Just find the boys!
Snack crumbs scatter on the floor,
Who's the culprit? We ask for more!

Board games turn into epic fights,
Strategic retreats to sleep at nights.
Laughter bursts like popcorn pop,
In this room, we can't seem to stop.

Thresholds of Connection

The doorbell rings, a surprise guest,
Uncle Joe comes in, and we're all blessed.
He tells dad jokes that make us groan,
But we can't help it, we call it home.

In the hallway, shoes line the floor,
Tripping hazards? Just ask for more!
Each room holds stories, secrets to share,
This is our stage, laughter fills the air.

Interwoven Footprints

The kitchen's a battleground of crumbs,
While Mom yells, "Who wants the drums?"
Dancing around in mismatched socks,
The dog joins in—oh, what a paradox!

A sponge fight breaks out during the clean,
Soap slips and slides, pure entertainment!
As we stumble over, we trip and we laugh,
Through all of this mess, we find our path.

Traces of Togetherness

In the kitchen, pots begin to dance,
Spaghetti twirls, oh what a chance!
Sauce splatters like a playful art,
Chaos and laughter blend from the start.

Socks hilariously stray from their pair,
A treasure hunt is beyond compare.
Under the couch, behind the shoe,
Finding them all is a sport, it's true!

Beneath the Same Ceiling

The cat claims the couch with regal pride,
While kids jump around with a comical glide.
One giggles, then trips, oh what a sight,
Laughter erupts in the warmth of the night.

The dog steals the blanket, the popcorn too,
A family fight over snacks, who knew?
With pillows as shields and laughter as arms,
This absurdity always has its charms.

Embracing the Collective

Fridge magnets clash, a wild art show,
A llama and taco, where did they go?
Juggling breakfast while hiding the coat,
Who knew chaos could float like a boat?

Banter and bickering, a symphony sweet,
One steals a fry, another's retreat.
Whispers of secrets brushed by the hand,
Building a fort, oh isn't it grand?

Notes of Familiarity

In the pile of laundry, a sock revolution,
Each item holds tales, it's a fun institution.
"Did you wash my shirt?" becomes a jest,
Every mishap feels like a fun quest.

Dance-offs in the hallway, a sight to behold,
Pretending to be rock stars, brave and bold.
All in good fun, we crash in a heap,
In this joyful mess, love runs deep.

Echoes in the Hallway

Footsteps dance on squeaky floors,
Laughter rolls from opened doors.
A cat strolls by, judging us all,
In this tiny kingdom, we stand tall.

Mismatched socks on every chair,
Who stole my snack? Not quite fair!
A family feud at the dinner table,
Who knows where the forks are? Such a fable!

The TV's on, yet no one's there,
Faint echoes of a silly dare.
Who made the mess in the living space?
Guess we should all just embrace grace!

Jokes fly like a zigzagging kite,
Who's winning the sarcasm fight?
Amid the chaos, love does grow,
Here's to the laughs, we steal the show.

The Unseen Threads

Threads of food spills on the floor,
Laundry battles, never a bore.
With tangled cords and mismatched plates,
We weave the fabric that creates fates.

Mornings lost in toast and jam,
The dog just stole Auntie Pam.
Chasing tails and dodging shoes,
In this circus, we can't lose!

A sitcom plays, but we just sigh,
Someone ate the last pie—oh, why?
Arguments over who left lights on,
Yet, in a heartbeat, the grumpiness is gone.

What binds us here is more than mess,
Love and laughter? Oh yes, no stress!
So raise your glass for all the fun,
Our quirky lives, never done!

Together Yet Apart

We gather close, yet drift apart,
In our own worlds, right from the start.
Like shadows in the kitchen bright,
Who's stealing snacks, who's lost in flight?

The remote's gone, who took it last?
Rewind to find our silly past.
Shared moments in a puzzle box,
Each piece crazier than old socks.

Together for a meal at six,
But lost in our weird Netflix picks.
A dinner table filled with glee,
Typical chaos—a sight to see!

Though we bicker, we truly care,
In this mad house, love fills the air.
So here's a toast (to zap the strife),
Together apart in this crazy life!

Where Hearts Converge

In this hive of buzzing fun,
Socks on the ceiling? Oh what a run!
We spin in circles, a merry chase,
In this busy world, we find our place.

Voices rise over clattering pans,
Yet laughter beats all the grand plans.
Mixing spices, blending souls,
In this chaos, our love rolls.

From midnight snacks to morning calls,
Tales of mishaps line the walls.
Game nights filled with playful jabs,
For every joke, we're the fab lab!

So let's embrace the quirks we hold,
In this mansion, hearts dare to bold.
Amidst the chaos, smiles emerge,
In this joyful mess, our hearts converge.

Embraced by Familiarity

In a house where socks go missing,
And the fridge hums a tune,
We dance around each other,
Like goats on a hot afternoon.

Laundry piles up like mountains,
With treasures we never locate,
Chasing down lost remotes,
It's a hilarious fate.

The dog steals the cushions,
With laughter filling the air,
As children plot their next prank,
Oh, the stories we share!

In kitchen chaos, we gather,
Making memories with cheer,
Each meal a funny adventure,
That's why we all are here.

The Footprints of Us

Footprints mark the hallway,
Where snacks lead the way,
To find the last cookie,
It's a treasure hunt play.

Whispers dance in the corners,
Secrets hidden in sight,
While socks form a parade,
In the dim evening light.

Chairs wobble and creak,
In our daily routine,
As we bicker and tease,
Like a comedic scene.

From silly faces at dinner,
To jokes that we spin,
Life's clumsy footprints,
Always tangled in kin.

A Sanctuary of Souls

A sanctuary filled with laughter,
Echoes down the hall,
With pranks that go too far,
A loveable free-for-all.

The cat claims her territory,
While the kids run amok,
Between juice spills and giggles,
Every day's quite the shock!

Mismatched shoes by the door,
Like a bizarre art piece,
Each step tells a story,
In this chaos, we find peace.

In a realm of joyous noise,
And hugs that last long,
We've built this funny fortress,
Where we all belong.

Tides of Togetherness

Waves of laughter crash here,
Like kids on the run,
Each day's a new adventure,
Under bright, blazing sun.

In the bubble of our world,
Silly arguments flow,
Like who gets the biggest slice,
Of the pizza we know.

Socks on the ceiling fan,
A sight to behold,
With giggles at breakfast,
Our tales truly unfold.

In the ebb and the flow,
We're a quirky kind of crew,
Finding joy in the madness,
In everything that we do.

The Embrace of Community

In a house where shoes collide,
And socks have nowhere to hide,
We dance to tunes, both loud and bright,
With laughter echoing into the night.

The fridge is packed with mystery meals,
A potluck feast that nobody feels,
The cat and dog share little space,
While kids zoom past in a wild race.

One sees a coat, the other a hat,
Found on the chair, but not on the mat,
Arguments over the TV remote,
Even the plants have learned to emote!

From morning coffee to late-night chats,
Boredom finds no time to chat,
With endless quirks in this crazy place,
We find our joy in the warm embrace.

A Dwelling of Dreams

In a place where dreams collide,
The couch is a ship, we take our ride,
Pillows as clouds, we float away,
In this universe, we all want to play.

Dishes pile with reckless cheer,
As we toast with juice or maybe beer,
The mop has retired, it's clearly stressed,
We've perfected the art of the cluttered nest!

With "Who left this here?", we start the day,
And "Can you find my shoe?", the usual fray,
But every giggle and every squabble,
Is a thread in our tapestry, a joyful hobble.

This home is a circus, a carnival too,
Where every jester brings something new,
In this bubbling pot of silly schemes,
Together we're chasing our wildest dreams.

Voices of Home

Here we chatter and shout, no doubt,
Each voice unique, like a wild route,
'Hey, where's my sandwich?' erupts from the stew,
While others debate the color of blue.

From spats over the best TV show,
To plotting how to sneak out and glow,
The echoes of joy fill up every nook,
As we team up for the ultimate cook.

When one's feeling moody or drifted away,
Another's right there with a neat ballet,
Jokes about socks and where they may run,
Life here's a sitcom, with laughter the sun.

With walls that shake from our hearty yells,
We mix our stories like colorful gels,
In this raucous blend of fun and sighs,
Home is our stage, dressed under bright skies.

Corners of Kindred

In corners where secrets are shared with glee,
And the big fuzzy blanket fits you and me,
We gather around for stories and snacks,
While hidden treasures peek from the cracks.

The elder tells tales of days gone by,
While the baby just giggles and gives it a try,
Between playful pokes and some friendly chides,
We build a fortress where love abides.

The plant on the shelf seems to join the fun,
With leaves that dance, it knows it's not done,
Amidst all the craziness, there's magic profound,
In the corners of kindness, our hearts are unbound.

Here's to the quirks that make us feel whole,
The laughter and chaos that tickle the soul,
In this delightful mix of our chosen crew,
Every moment's a treasure, every heart beats true.

Echoing Laughter

In the kitchen, pots and pans do dance,
A clatter here, a splatter there, it's pure chance.
The dog runs off with one of my socks,
And grandma chases him—what a paradox!

Caught in the hallway, I hear a loud shout,
My brother stole my sandwich; I have no doubt!
While dad keeps telling the same old joke,
Mom rolls her eyes, but we all just choke.

When it's movie night, remote in dispute,
Arguments fly, each side is so astute.
But popcorn's flying, laughter fills the air,
At the end of the night, we pretend we don't care.

The bathroom's busy; I can't make a move,
Foot tapping wildly; will I ever win this groove?
Yet as the door swings wide and giggles ensue,
We all squeeze in, and it's a silly view!

Ties that Bind

My sister steals my clothes; I'm left in despair,
Yet at least she's stylish—there's joy in that flair.
Jokes about laundry mix with the scent,
As we hunt for the missing sock in the dent!

The fridge is a puzzle, a Tetris game,
Finding leftovers? It feels like a shame.
I ask who made this questionable stew,
Dad shrugs with a grin—could it be you?

When game night strikes, the air fills with cheer,
But an argument starts as we rotate the beer.
Who picks the game? It's a fight to the death,
Yet somehow we laugh until we're out of breath.

We dub this chaos our wild, crazy fate,
Kisses and hugs balance food on our plate.
In this merry mess, we all still confide,
With countless giggles, our hearts swell with pride!

Whispers of Belonging

In the early mornings, when coffee's our friend,
I tiptoe past the cat, hoping she won't offend.
Sister's still snoring, a delightful view,
Her hair's a wild tangle; is that a bird too?

With music blaring, we dance in the hall,
Uncoordinated moves make us all look small.
Dad busts a groove, it's a sight to behold,
While mom spices it up, as her laughter unfolds.

Sharing secrets beneath blankets piled high,
We whisper sweet nonsense, as time flutters by.
A tickle here, a punch there, it's all in good fun,
Playing hide and seek till the day is all done.

Sunday's a circus; who'll cook and who'll clean?
Mismatched socks dancing, a colorful scene.
Yet love fills the air, amid quirks and delight,
In this wild little nest, our hearts take flight!

The Closeness of Strangers

There's always a mix-up with names and with faces,
A neighbor pops by, steals comfortable spaces.
We laugh at the chaos, we step on each other,
And yet in this madness, we're more like a brother.

In the living room, debates get intense,
Who brewed this coffee? It's so very dense!
Dad claims it's an art, while we disagree,
But with every sip, there's a giggle and glee.

When friends drop by and the couch gets too full,
We squeeze like sardines; isn't that the rule?
The pizza arrives, as if summoned by fate,
We're one big mess, but oh, it's first-rate!

Plans for tomorrow get tossed 'round in jest,
"What if we camp in the backyard, be our best?"
Yet through dusty ideas and giggles galore,
We build our own home, forever encore!

Reflections in Our Walls

In the kitchen, crumbs do dance,
Spilled milk meets a wobbly chance.
The fridge hums tunes, a quirky band,
While socks play hide and seek on command.

In the hall, echoes of our bickering,
Who left the lights on? That's what we're figuring.
Loud laughter bursts, like popcorn popping,
As laundry baskets keep on swapping.

Dinner time's a circus, plates as flying discs,
While dad tells tales of his epic risks.
Mom pretends to roll her eyes on demand,
But secretly, she loves the chaos that's grand.

From the bathroom, war cries flow,
"Who stole my shampoo?" Oh, the drama goes!
We wave our flags, all in good cheer,
Each day a new laugh, oddly sincere.

Comfort in the Chaos

Amidst the clutter, a comfy chair waits,
Books and toys, mixed like our fates.
The cat, the king, surveys his realm,
While chaos and laughter are at the helm.

Dishes pile high, a tower in sight,
"Who's washing? Not me!" is the family's light.
Yet somehow, in mess, there lies a spark,
The way we dance through the noise, not dark.

Remote controls lost in the couch's embrace,
Who knew, a game would turn into a race?
With snacks all shared, and stories to tell,
In this whirlwind, we're doing quite well.

Through peels of laughter, we all collide,
Hugs in abundance and hearts open wide.
In the lovely madness, we find our chore,
This is the joy, always yearning for more.

Bound by Four Walls

Four walls surround us, yet we roam free,
Like squirrels at play in a chaotic tree.
Each corner hides stories, some loud, some meek,
A journey of laughter, no need to speak.

The bathroom sings louder than a band,
With showers of steam and soap in hand.
Each child a pirate, searching for treasure,
While grown-ups revive their youthful leisure.

Our couch's a ship, with cushions as sails,
We set off for adventures, and never fail.
As we bounce and tumble, dreams take flight,
In our fortress of fun, hearts feel light.

Dinner is served, a banquet of glee,
With each bite shared, there's joy, can't you see?
In small, silly battles and family brawls,
We thrive in this wonder of four silly walls.

The Pulse of Coexistence

In the living room, wild antics unfold,
Jokes ricochet off the walls, loud and bold.
A game of charades turns into a scene,
With dad in a wig, he's a dramatic queen!

The kitchen's a lab, experiments gone wrong,
Flour on faces, we laugh all night long.
With pots as our instruments, we create a tune,
This orchestra welcomes the lights of the moon.

As bedtime approaches, the tales we share,
A dracula's romance or a bear in despair.
We giggle and squeal, each story a hit,
In this vibrant pulse, we find our true grit.

In pillows piled high, we dream of our fates,
Each heartbeat a dance, as chaos awaits.
Together we flourish, adore the embrace,
In this joyful mess, we find our true place.

Common Grounds

In a kitchen packed like sardines,
Each meal sparks laughter and scenes.
Spilled milk, a dog dashes by,
As leftovers take to the sky.

We share socks but not the fries,
In this circus, no room for sighs.
The fridge hums a tune of its own,
While we argue over last week's scone.

Chasing each other down the halls,
In a game that leads to epic falls.
We dodge, we duck, as chaos ensues,
Life's little battles, no time to snooze.

With quirks and giggles, we collide,
In this haven where joy can't hide.
Raise a toast to the funny and odd,
In this space, we're all just a bit flawed.

The Heartbeat of Home

Bickering about the thermostat,
Each side claims a cozy habitat.
One's too hot, the other's too cold,
Why's it always a battle so bold?

Laundry's a treasure hunt, it's true,
Matching socks? That's a myth too!
Found a sandwich from the last week's feast,
Now we're naming it, to say the least.

The TV blares our favorite shows,
With bickering on who really knows.
Popcorn flies, a kernel attack,
As laughter echoes, who would hold back?

Together we stand, in the silliest way,
Moments that boggle, but brighten our day.
Through chaos and fun, we keep it real,
In this heartbeat, it's love that we feel.

Where Paths Converge

In the hallway, we trip and tumble,
All while trying not to grumble.
A game of tag in a tight space,
Who knew home had such a fast pace?

Bathroom waits turn into lengthy lore,
With tales of woe, we can't ignore.
Fighting for space, it's all in good fun,
Who knew hygiene could be such a run?

A secret dance-off in the living room,
With socks sliding, we jive and zoom.
Sometimes we clash like thunder and rain,
But laughter rushes in to ease the strain.

In each corner, a story unfolds,
As laughter and mischief our life upholds.
Here's to moments, both silly and bright,
Where paths converge, it's a joyous sight.

Threads of Connection

Weave together snacks and tales,
Where pranks and giggles never fail.
This kinship stitched with golden threads,
As silly chaos leaps from our beds.

Who left the cap off the ketchup jar?
That's the start of a family spar!
Each spat may seem like a circus scene,
But it's all in love, if you know what I mean.

Dance parties break out at odd times,
With off-key singing and silly rhymes.
Each note a thread in our quirky quilt,
Stitched with laughter, and none of the guilt.

So here's to the threads that bind us tight,
In the midst of chaos, it feels just right.
With each shared moment, we paint our day,
In this funny fabric, let's laugh and play.

The Mingle of Lives

In the morning rush, socks are a pair,
But somehow, I find one on a chair.
A dance of breakfast, toast on the fly,
And who left the milk? Oh my, oh my!

The dog steals a shoe, the cat takes a seat,
While kids chase their dreams on tiny little feet.
We trip over laughter; we stumble on fun,
In this quirky circus, we're never outdone.

Like crumbs on the floor and toys in the hall,
We share all our secrets, both big and small.
Between mismatched dishes and half-empty cups,
We're a jigsaw puzzle with missing parts ups.

At night we all gather, a wild little crew,
With stories and snorts, each one something new.
Under this roof where chaos holds sway,
We wouldn't trade it — not now, not today.

Footsteps in Harmony

In the hallway, shoes are not quite a team,
One's a flip-flop; the other, a dream.
With giggles and squeals, we run up and down,
This house thinks it's big, but it's wearing a frown.

Each room holds a secret, a tale of its own,
From cereal spills to a pet's undertone.
The bathroom's a stage for performances grand,
While dishes in the sink play an un-washed band.

The light sometimes flickers, the fridge sings a song,
As roommates collide where chaos belongs.
A hats-off salute to the daily parade,
Life's rhythm in rushes, a dance we have made.

When the day winds down, and silence draws near,
We smile over moments and drink up the cheer.
With feet intertwined, we find our own beat,
Together we laugh, so here's to our seat!

Collective Shadows

Beneath this roof of shadows and light,
We fumble in darkness, but somehow, it's bright.
With pillows for forts and laughter like rain,
We dodge the odd tantrums and vagaries of pain.

The laundry pile grows, a mountain of woes,
But in the mess, our humor still flows.
From socks on the ceiling to crumbs in the chairs,
Even kitchen disasters become our best fairs.

We dance through the day with a rhythm so wild,
Like kids from the street, improvising, beguiled.
The pets are the judges, the snacks our reward,
In this grand spectacle, no one's left ignored.

As night falls, shadows start making their rounds,
Tales turn from laughter to the softest sounds.
Here's to the moments that keep us aligned,
In the beautiful chaos, our hearts are entwined.

A Nest of Narratives

In kitchen corners where whispers collide,
Stories unfold as our shadows confide.
With flour on noses and smiles in the air,
We cook up adventures, each one quite rare.

The coffee comes first, a ritual divine,
While socks dance together, an odd little line.
The doorbell's a trumpet of chaos and cheer,
As friends add their tales to the ones we hold dear.

In the living room jungle, the cushions are tossed,
We navigate currents where friendships embossed.
Our laughter in echoes, a harmony grand,
With bickering banter as our daily plan.

At dusk we all gather, a cozy warm space,
No room for gloom in this merry embrace.
With tales intertwined and hearts feeling light,
In this nest of narratives, we take flight!

The Palette of Coexistence

In our cozy space, socks disappear,
Whose is that shirt? Oh dear, oh dear!
The cat plots chaos, oh what a show,
While we juggle snacks and the remote, you know.

The kitchen's a canvas of culinary dreams,
Mixing leftovers, bursting at the seams.
Dishwasher battles, who does the chore?
Arguments over pizza, yet we adore!

Out in the living room, laughter erupts,
Who left the lights on? Those silly pups!
We share our quirks, preferences clear,
Like who steals the blankets? Oh, what a year!

In this hodgepodge of joy, we find our groove,
Each silly moment helps us to move.
Though chaos reigns, love is the glue,
In this madcap dance, I'll always choose you.

Our Shared Retreat

Our sanctuary's small, but big on flair,
Who ate the last cookie? Let's pause and stare.
Living with mishaps, we curtail the stress,
Barking orders at pets, what a mess!

The fridge is packed, like a treasure trove,
Exploring each shelf, with mystery to probe.
Leftover pizza? Oh, what a delight!
Dinner plans forgotten, yet all feels right.

We step on Legos; oh, what a pinch,
The battle for remote, just a tiny clinch.
Yet here in our nest, with quirks on display,
We mix up our lives in a comical way.

With every loud laugh, we forge our way,
Resilience and giggles make every day.
In this quirky retreat, love's the best part,
Even if we're not perfect, you have my heart.

Sharing Light

In our shared abode, the coffee runs wild,
A morning misadventure of dreams as a child.
Who moved the lamp? I need some light!
Navigating chaos feels just so right.

Each room's a gallery, painted with quirks,
Visual symphonies of lovable jerks.
From dance-offs in kitchens to pillow fights,
Creating our humor through sleepless nights.

The WiFi's a wonder, never quite strong,
Yet streaming together, we sing our song.
In harmony's chaos, our lives intertwine,
Through laughter and mishaps, your heart's next to mine.

So here's to the days, both messy and bright,
In this circus of joy, you make it all right.
Together we shine, a comedic delight,
In our cozy little world, everything's light.

The Confluence of Hearts

A melting pot bubbling with laughter and cheer,
We gather 'round, no need to adhere.
Whose turn is it now for the bathroom line?
Our regal throne struggles to stay divine.

We battle for snacks, and we argue for fun,
But sharing the joy means we've already won.
Fridge poetry written in ketchup and cheese,
Crafting our epics with so much ease!

When life's little quirks collide with our ways,
We anticipate mishaps, and join in the play.
Life's rollercoaster twist keeps our hearts bold,
Through spats and giggles, our story unfolds.

So let's raise a toast to our delightful grind,
In this humorous whirlwind, together we find,
A family of friends, each varied and sweet,
In the confluence of hearts, our lives are complete.

Nightfall on the Shared Path

In the kitchen, pans collide,
As snacks abound, our joys can't hide.
The fridge hums loudly, what a tune,
Dance breaks happen, and we swoon!

In the hallway, socks misplace,
One's a bear, the other's face.
Loud arguments over shows we binge,
Each opinion makes the room fringe.

The bathroom line is quite the feat,
Who took the last roll? Oh, what a cheat!
We laugh and groan, this tension bright,
Together we jest, it feels just right.

As night falls in this cozy spot,
We ponder how we share a lot.
With laughter echoing through each room,
Even chaos finds a way to bloom.

Collective Reverie

Mismatched plates on the table lie,
From ages past, oh my, oh my!
We laugh at dinners, spilled on clothes,
Sharing secrets that everyone knows.

The remote's a tug of war each week,
Who gets to choose? The stakes are bleak!
We flip and flop 'til we agree,
On a movie that's pure comedy.

Laundry battles on the weekend drum,
Fighting for space, oh, what a hum!
Socks are warriors in the fray,
But hey, they find a home someday.

In this wild mix of love and fuss,
We thrive in shouts, in joyful fuss.
With laughter lifting us so high,
Who knew chaos could touch the sky?

Harmony in Shared Spaces

In the living room, we all collide,
With games and laughter, side by side.
The cat observes this wild display,
As we make memories day by day.

In the kitchen, spices fight for fame,
While dinner arguments spark a flame.
We burn toast and laugh at the scene,
It's a culinary comedy routine!

The garden blooms with quirky blooms,
We pull weeds and share the grooms.
In the chaos, we plant our dreams,
Watered by laughter, bursting at the seams.

As evening drapes its cozy cloth,
We bond through jokes and playful sloth.
In this shared space, joy cannot flee,
Together we thrive, just wait and see!

Beneath the Same Sky

Under the stars, we shout and cheer,
Tales of the day, good grief, oh dear!
With every story told so grand,
We laugh until we can barely stand.

In the backyard, a BBQ mess,
Charcoal smoke leads to much distress.
We toast the burgers with a snort,
Each burnt bite, a comic report.

Game nights bring out competition,
Who wins? It's sheer superstition!
We toss the dice and groan at fate,
But in defeat, we celebrate.

As laughter shifts to sleepy sighs,
We share our dreams beneath the skies.
With our quirky band of misfits near,
This funny life, we hold so dear.

The Balance of Coexistence

In a house full of quirks, we navigate,
Dodging socks left behind, it's never too late.
One loves to cook, the other to eat,
With chaos and laughter, life feels complete.

The cat steals the chair, it's quite the sight,
A dog steals the food, causing a slight fight.
Comedies unfold at the dinner table,
As we share our woes, and sometimes, a fable.

The fridge is a puzzle, what's mine, what's thine?
Whose sauce is that? Oh wait, it's all fine.
We laugh through the mess, each quirk is our song,
Together we bloom, where all can belong.

In our cozy chaos, we find delight,
From midnight snacks to the morning light.
Though we may argue about the remote,
In this wild, shared space, we truly emote.

Interwoven Dreams

In a symphony of snoring, each night begins,
One likes it quiet, the other spins.
Between tangled sheets, and wayward limbs,
Dreams collide softly, laughter brims.

The alarm clock blasts at a scandalous hour,
One hits snooze, like a sleepy flower.
Groans fill the air as the day starts anew,
Cereal and chaos, our shared morning view.

The living room doubles as a battleground,
With toys and dirty socks strewn all around.
Blurry-eyed mornings lead to coffee spills,
Yet even the mess, our goodwill instills.

We dance through the chaos, a twirl and a spin,
In this theatrical home, we all fit in.
So here's to our dreams, interwoven and bright,
Together we blossom, in laughter and light.

Touchstones of Unity

In the heart of the home lies a trio of hearts,
One snorts when she laughs, that's just how it starts.
The other two giggle, they join in the spree,
This motley crew thrives, living wild and free.

The dishwasher's a monster, it howls on the side,
While we bicker about who'll take out the fried.
Yet at the end of the day, we gather 'round late,
Sharing tales of the funny, we simply create.

Our differences clash, like noodles and sauce,
But there's always a truce, we're not at a loss.
It's the quirks that we cherish, they help us unite,
In the cosmic dance of our own delight.

So let's raise a toast, with mugs held up high,
To the laughter and love that never runs dry.
For in this bond, the hilarity reigns,
Celebrating life in all of its plains.

Secrets in Shared Silences

In the quiet moments, where mischief brews,
Sneaky glances exchanged, laughter ensues.
The pizza guy knows us, our simple delight,
As we barter for slices through late, sneaky nights.

In the corners we find, peculiar little things,
A treasure of secrets that each laughter brings.
Hidden snacks stashed, like artifacts rare,
We giggle in whispers, without a care.

When words fail us, the silence will sing,
Echoing laughter in the joy of spring.
Unexpected pranks, like a gate swung too wide,
These moments together, we cannot divide.

So let's revel in what makes us a team,
In silence and humor, we boldly dream.
With eyes that twinkle, and smirks that are sly,
We create a bond that will never say bye.

Gathering of Souls

In the kitchen, my brother steals my snack,
While the cat plans its sneak attack.
Mom yells, "Who left the door ajar?"
As Dad trips on the old guitar.

In the living room, we bump and jive,
A dance party where all survive.
Laughter rings as we step on toes,
Chasing the dog who just struck a pose.

At dinner, we argue over sides,
Who's the best cook? Oh, how pride divides!
Yet, smiles emerge with every bite,
Together we stand, arm in arm, ready for night.

With tales that stretch, we share pure glee,
In this space, we're wild and free.
Through chaos and fun, our hearts find cheer,
In laughter and love, we persevere.

The Art of Togetherness

In a house where socks disappear,
We search and laugh, not a hint of fear.
Who stole the remote? It causes a fight,
Yet gathered we stay till the end of night.

The bathroom's a race, a daily affair,
Teeth brushing clashes, who doesn't care?
With two in line, it's a comic scream,
Each morning's a show, a funny routine.

In the backyard, our barbecues sizzle,
A master chef winks, flips with a drizzle.
But when burgers burn, the laughter erupts,
As we make new plans for future cup-ups.

Family game nights can sure bring a fright,
As dice roll wild, and tempers ignite.
Yet in every chaos, joy doth abide,
In this madcap circus, love's our guide.

Unified by Walls

Four humans with quirks, a peculiar mix,
Like a jigsaw puzzle, we fit with quirks and fix.
One's a night owl, the other a spry morn,
In this lively chaos, true bonds are born.

In the hallway, the shoes pile high,
"Did you trip over that?" we slyly reply.
With mismatched socks and slippers galore,
We giggle at life; who could ask for more?

Each room a realm, with characters bold,
One hoarding books, while another's ice cold.
In our little world, the rules are our own,
As we dance through this house, a love has grown.

When quiet moments flare, it's often a jest,
Who forgot to clean up? Let's face the test!
In tales that we weave, hilarity's key,
Together we thrive as a wild family.

Under One Canopy

A roof above us, with tales to tell,
Of sneaky snacks and the toilet seat spell.
It's a circus of joy, this playful scene,
In the heart of the home, we reign like a queen.

When one takes a nap, the rest plot and scheme,
Whispers of tricks, and we chase a dream.
With pillows as shields, we fight like knights,
This fortress of fun fills our days and nights.

Laundry mountains rise, it's a chore we dread,
Yet, fashionably wrinkled, we all forge ahead.
A game of hide and seek in the pile,
"Who wore that?" we laugh, "Let's stay for a while!"

As seasons change, our antics evolve,
Every hiccup in life, together we solve.
In this crazy home, our hearts stay neat,
United like ninjas, in joy we compete.

In the Company of Shadows

In the kitchen, pots all clatter,
Cats are plotting, what's the matter?
Whiskers twitch, they think they're sly,
While the toast begins to fly.

On the couch, we share the space,
Remote control, a tricky race.
Who will claim the last snack pack?
Tug of war, and then it's back!

Laughter echoes down the hall,
Who left crumbs and made the call?
Chaos reigns, but it's okay,
We love this merry, silly way.

In every room, there's a dance,
Clumsy moves, no second chance.
Together we are quite a sight,
A jumbled joy, oh what a night!

Nestled in Unity

In the morning, snooze alarms,
Fluffy blankets, cozy arms.
Coffee spills and laughter flows,
Who's the last to wake? Who knows!

At the table, food galore,
Pancakes stacked, and then some more.
Syrup rivers, syrup seas,
Sticky fingers bring us glee.

Outside, the garden's quite a sight,
We plant the seeds—yeah, that's just right!
But weeds grow high, plants go shy,
Did we forget? Oh my, oh my!

At the end of each wild day,
We share our tales, come what may.
Our little tribe, all sorts of fun,
Nestled close, we're never done!

Fragments of Togetherness

In the hallway, shoes in piles,
Navigating through the smiles.
Each corner packed with quirky bits,
Forgotten toys and silly skits.

In the bathroom, bubbles fly,
Rubber ducks say "Oh my, oh my!"
The toddler splashes, giggles loud,
Clean-up crew? Not a chance allowed!

Chasing thoughts with snacks in hand,
Discussion turns to cookie brand.
A war over the last cheese stick—
Victory dance! Now that's the trick!

As night falls, we gather near,
Sharing dreams, and a hearty cheer.
In this happy, messy dance,
Together is our greatest chance!

A Symphony of Footsteps

In the living room, a tune does play,
Dancing feet in a silly way.
Who knew that socks could take on flight,
Spinning round until the night!

Siblings giggle, duck and weave,
Hide and seek, we can't believe!
In the pantry, sneaky hands,
Raiding treasure, quick as bands!

Spotted crumbs lead us astray,
"Who made dinner?" we survey.
Pasta bowls and laughter fill,
Spaghetti art? What a thrill!

Time to rest, the day's been grand,
With every smile, we understand.
Together, oh what a sight we make,
A symphony of joy, that's no mistake!

The Pulse of Togetherness

We dance in our socks, a sight so absurd,
While dodging the cat, who silently stirred.
The fridge hums a tune, familiar and sweet,
As we argue on who claimed the last slice of meat.

Chaos unfolds, laughter fills the air,
Remote controls vanish, does anyone care?
We write our own rules, in silly debates,
And share all our quirks, despite our odd traits.

Morning brings coffee, spills on the floor,
While cereal rains down as we search for more.
The chaos is normal, a beautiful hell,
In this whirlwind of life, we manage quite well.

At night we connect, rehashing the day,
In our mismatched pajamas, we giggle and play.
With stories and snacks, the fun never ends,
In this crazy abode, we're forever best friends.

Garden of Shared Dreams

In the backyard we dream, with flowers and weeds,
Trying to grow veggies; a work that exceeds.
We fight over soil, and who's got the best,
But end up just talking while we relax and rest.

The sun turns to dusk, our plans all a mess,
With mulch on our clothes, it's anyone's guess.
Yet laughter erupts, while we gather our tools,
Planting our hopes in this paradise of fools.

Neighbors peek over, some giving a grin,
"Are they planting a garden or just having a kin?"
We wave and we laugh, as we dig and we joke,
In our own little world, from worries we poke.

Come every spring, we fill up the air,
With stories of triumph, and some that we share.
In this garden of dreams, where joy seems to bloom,
We grow not just plants, but laughter and room.

Moments of Synchronicity

We wake up at six, it's a synchronized fate,
To step on each other, oh isn't it great?
Breakfast chaos, with toast everywhere,
We bump and we fumble in our sleepy despair.

The bathroom's a warzone, who's in there too long?
We argue, we laugh, as we hum a quick song.
Outfits collide, does it matter, who knows?
In our web of confusion, hilarity flows.

Lunch breaks are madness, we share a small plate,
"Is that my last fry?" "No, just wait, contemplate!"
We bicker, we mock, yet it's all in good fun,
This ballet of life, oh, we've barely begun.

As night wraps us gently in stories and snorts,
We constellate memories, in colorful sorts.
In moments of chaos, a rhythm we find,
With shared little quirks that keep us entwined.

A Patchwork of Stories

Each wall holds a tale, each room has a voice,
From laughter to losses, it's our little choice.
We patch up old quilt squares, sewn with our dreams,
In this goofy abode, where nothing's as it seems.

The dog steals my socks, what a cheeky old guy,
While the kids share their secrets, with giggles they fly.
In messes we blend, like colors so bright,
Every spilled drink brings an hour of delight.

Dinner table stories, too wild to be true,
As we toss all our humor like confetti for two.
With plates piled high and the jokes flowing free,
We savor each moment, our own comedy spree.

When twilight descends, we gather around,
With tales of the day, our laughter resounds.
In this patchwork of life, woven with cheer,
We stitch together memories, year after year.

www.ingramcontent.com/pod-product-compliance
Lightning Source LLC
Chambersburg PA
CBHW070005300426
43661CB00141B/234